SHRED IT!

TAKE A DIVE

EXTREME CLIFF DIVING

Virginia Loh-Hagan

45th Parallel Press

Ann Arbor, Michigan

www.cherrylakepublishing.com

Content Adviser: Liv Williams, Editor, iLivExtreme

Reading Adviser: Beth Walker Gambro, MS, Ed., Reading Consultant, Yorkville, IL

Photo Credits: © EpicStockMedia/Shutterstock, cover, title page; © URS FLUEELER/EPA-EFE/Shutterstock, 5; © Juergen Nowak/Shutterstock, 6; © Juanma Aparicio/Alamy, 7; © Dennis MacDonald/Shutterstock, 9; © David Fleetham/Alamy, 11; © Antonin Albert/Shutterstock, 12; © enginakyurt/Shutterstock, 13; © KAleksandr0909/Shutterstock, 15; © Nic Randall/Shutterstock, 16; © Mario Hagen/Shutterstock, 18; © EpicStockMedia/Shutterstock, 21; © A.Taoualit/Shutterstock, 22; © Travel Pix/Alamy, 25; © Insidefoto/Alamy, 26–27; © maliprinc11/Shutterstock, 28; © Kathryn Sullivan/Shutterstock, 29

Library of Congress Cataloging-in-Publication Data has been filed and is available at catalog.loc.gov

Cherry Lake Press would like to acknowledge the work of the Partnership for 21st Century Learning, a Network of Battelle for Kids. Please visit Battelle for Kids online for more information.

Printed in the United States of America

Note from publisher: Websites change regularly, and their future contents are outside of our control. Supervise children when conducting any recommended online searches for extended learning opportunities.

ABOUT THE AUTHOR

Virginia Loh-Hagan is an author, university professor, former classroom teacher, and curriculum designer. In college, she jumped off a bunk bed and broke her toe. No more jumping for her. She lives in San Diego with her very tall husband and very naughty dogs.

Table of Contents

CHAPTER 1

Diving In

Ginger Huber went to the end of the cliff. She took a deep breath. She relaxed her shoulders. She trusted herself. She knew what she was doing.

She didn't have time to count to 3. She didn't want to change her mind. She dived. Her rear end faced the water. She couldn't see the water. She straightened out her body just before she hit the surface. She barely made a splash.

This move is the Flying Front. Huber won awards for it. She did it in the Red Bull Cliff Diving World Series. Huber trained. She needed high cliffs. She had to drive to faraway places. She found a way.

Ginger Huber at a Red Bull Cliff Diving World Series competition in Lake Lucerne, Sisikon, Switzerland

Cliff divers, like Huber, jump from high places. They jump from cliffs. They jump from diving towers. They dive fast into water. Cliff divers do their tricks early in the dive. Their flight is about 3 seconds long. Then they prepare their bodies. They get in proper positions to hit the water.

SHRED IT! SPOTLIGHT BIOGRAPHY:

Orlando Duque

Orlando Duque is "The Duke" of cliff diving. He is a legend. He won 13 world titles. He set 2 world records. He's from Colombia. He started at age 9. First, he dived in swimming pools. He did Olympic-style diving. But he grew tired of pools. He needed more of a challenge. So he dived off cliffs. He said, "When I'm standing up on top, I'm worried. I know this is high. It's going to be some danger involved in the dive. But I still want to do it...In three seconds you went from being really worried and now you're in the water and you're super happy. It just changes really quickly and it's hard to compare to anything else." Duque's cliff diving career lasted more than 20 years. He retired from competitive cliff diving in 2019. He said, "Cliff diving is my profession, a calling that will be the center of my life after my active career is over...It will never release its hold over me."

ORLANDO DUQUE

Cliff diving is a **precision** sport. Precision means being exact. Cliff divers must have perfect timing. They study the cliffs. They study **obstacles**, or objects, that could get in the way. They study water depths. They study **tides**. They calculate distances. They study the angle and speed of hitting water. One mistake means injury or death.

That's what cliff diving is all about. Cliff divers face the danger. They practice. They challenge themselves. They take the leap!

Cliff diving is different from Olympic platform diving. Olympic platform divers jump from about 33 feet (10 m) high. They hit the water hands first at about 30 miles (48 km) per hour. Competitive cliff divers jump from cliffs 66 to 92 feet (20 to 28 m) high. They hit the water feet first at over 60 miles (96.5 km) per hour.

In cliff diving, form is everything.

CHAPTER 2

Cliff Diving: Past to Present

Cliff diving began in the late 1700s in Hawaii. King Kahekili jumped off a 70-foot (21-m) cliff. He jumped into **sacred** waters. Sacred means special or holy. He became known as "Birdman." He set an example for his warriors. His warriors jumped. They proved their bravery. They proved their loyalty.

Later, King Kamehameha perfected lele kawa. This is jumping feetfirst without making a splash. Locals began cliff diving. Kamehameha turned cliff diving into a competition. He judged the style of the dive. He judged the amount of splash.

The World High Diving Federation formed in 1996. It promotes cliff diving. It organizes competitions. It created guidelines for judging.

King Kahekili took his historic leap from these cliffs on the island of Lanai in Hawaii.

Officials judge the **takeoff**. This is when cliff divers jump. They judge the tricks done in the air. They judge **somersaults** and twists. Somersaults are complete flips. They judge entry into the water.

Red Bull hosts the Cliff Diving World Series. It established this competition in 2009. Cliff divers participate in several events. They jump from platforms 85 to 92 feet (26 to 28 m) high. The champion scores the highest number of points.

Red Bull Cliff Diving World Series competitions draw huge crowds. The competition in Polignano a Mare, Italy, in 2025 had 35,000 fans. But the 2019 Dún Laoghaire, Ireland, competition set records. There were 145,000 fans in attendance! People love watching cliff diving.

EXTREME CLIFF DIVING:

Know the Lingo

Back group: dives where the diver jumps off and rotates backward

Barani: a somersault with a half twist

Blind entry: entering the water without seeing it, such as by diving backward

Flying: starting the dive in a straight position, then moving into a tuck or pike

Free: dives where the diver includes twists and uses more than one body position (straight, pike, or tuck)

Front group: dives where the diver jumps off and rotates forward

Inward group: dives where the diver faces the platform and jumps backward, then rotates forward

Pike: a body position with the legs straight and the body bent at the hips

Reverse group: dives where the diver starts facing the water and rotates backward during the dive

Straight: flight position with no bend in the hips or knees

Tuck: flight position with the body folded up in a tight ball

Twist group: dives where the diver does one or more twists in the air

PIKE POSITION

CHAPTER 3

There's a Style for Every Diver!

There are different types of cliff diving. Divers choose what they think is more fun. They choose what they think is more thrilling.

ROPE JUMPING

Extreme jumpers developed rope jumping. It combines cliff diving and rock climbing. It's dangerous.

Rope jumpers use harnesses when they jump off cliffs. They use ropes. These ropes do not stretch. The ropes stop divers close to the water or ground.

TOMBSTONING

Tombstoning is another type of cliff diving. A **tombstone** is a large, flat stone. It marks a grave. Cliff divers jump from high places. They try to enter the water feet first. They keep their bodies straight like tombstones.

Tombstoning got popular with social media. Untrained divers jumped from high places. They liked the **adrenaline** they got. Adrenaline is a hormone. Bodies release it in times of stress or excitement. Untrained divers can hit the water wrong. Many have died. Many have been paralyzed.

MIDO
Red Bull
T Mobile
Red Bull

Technical cliff diving is all about control. Divers perform dive **routines**. Routines are series of repeated movements. Technical divers are highly trained. Many practice for years. They enter competitions. They jump from cliffs or platforms. They earn points for completing their diving routines.

TECHNICAL
CLIFF DIVING

FREESTYLE
CLIFF DIVING

With freestyle cliff diving, divers can get creative. It's more like an art form. Divers don't have to follow a set routine. They don't have to do specific tricks.

Freestyle cliff divers have fun inventing and mastering new tricks. They tuck, flip, and spin. They do different combinations of tricks. Divers don't all have the same style. It's free. It's flexible.

Red Bull
budgy
smuggle

SHRED IT!
ADVICE FROM THE FIELD:
Rhiannan Iffland

Rhiannan Iffland is a cliff diver from Australia. She has won the Red Bull Cliff Diving World Series 8 times, including in 2025! But her first cliff diving competition didn't go well. She had to be pulled from the water by a safety diver. After that, Iffland was nervous about competing again. Her dad gave her some good advice. He said, "Well you know it's only up from here. You had a bad competition... just go there, enjoy it, and trust the process. Trust what you've done." This advice helped Iffland feel more confident. She hasn't looked back since. She kept challenging herself to reach new goals. She jumped from helicopters. She jumped from the mast of a huge ship. She jumped from a hot air balloon. She even dove from a platform in a cave 394 feet (120 m) underground. Iffland is enjoying cliff diving and trusting the process, just like her dad told her. It's only up from here!

RHIANNAN IFFLAND

CHAPTER 4

Keep Shredding!

Cliff diving can cause injury or death. Cliff divers prepare for danger. They check the cliffs. They check the landing space. The water can be dangerous. **Currents** are fast-moving streams of water. They can pull cliff divers under. Some water is not clear. Cliff divers can't see obstacles.

Cliff divers travel at extreme speeds for a short period of time. **Impact** with the water can be dangerous. Impact is the force of hitting something. Water is not a cushion. It can feel like concrete at high speeds. It can compress spines. It can break bones.

Divers must know what they are diving into.

But many people are trying to cliff dive as safely as possible. This is the spirit of extreme cliff diving. A balance of safety and risk is what makes the sport fun.

One cliff diver keeping this in mind is Aidan Heslop. He is from Wales, in the United Kingdom. He is the youngest person ever to win the Red Bull Cliff Diving World Series. He did this in 2024 at age 22.

Heslop has talked about how he took more risks when he was a teenager. But now, "there's more caution around the safety involved to keep [his] body as healthy as it can be in and ready for the big impact of the dive." He sat out the first event of the 2025 season to help his body heal from a spinal injury. Safety first!

Safety includes knowing where it is safe to jump and training your body to hit the water correctly.

Extreme cliff divers encourage their friends to be safe. They continue working hard to make their sport better.

SHRED IT!

When Extreme Is Too Extreme!

Imagine cliff diving with ghosts! Waimea Falls is in Hawaii. It's believed to be haunted. Many cliff divers have died there. Most of these cliff divers were non-Hawaiians. The falls drop 45 feet (13.7 m). A local legend says that a god slipped and fell from the cliff. This created the falls. The god lives at the bottom of the pool. The god wants sacrifices. Cliff divers whose bodies didn't surface were believed to be taken by the god. Legend says the god would eventually release the bodies. The bodies would wash to shore. In some photos, people say they can see a ghost cliff diver diving beside live cliff divers. At low tide, some people say they can see a skeleton shape made out of the cliff's rocks. They believe the god is warning people to stay away. Cliff diving was once banned. But today, professional cliff divers perform there.

WAIMEA FALLS IN O'AHU, HAWAII

DID YOU KNOW?

- Orlando Duque once landed on a bird. The bird flew under him just as he hit the water.
- Casa Bonita is a famous restaurant in Denver, Colorado. It hires cliff divers. It has a 30-foot (9-m) waterfall. Cliff divers dive every 15 minutes for 6 hours. Customers eat Mexican food while watching the divers.
- Diver Justin Shiigi wears shark costumes when he dives off 50-foot (15-m) cliffs.
- Beginning divers should wear water or diving shoes. These help protect against impact.

CONSIDER THIS!

TAKE A POSITION! Guinness World Records no longer tracks cliff diving. The organization thinks it's too dangerous. They don't want to support cliff diving. Why do you think this is the case? Do you agree or disagree with this position? Argue your point with reasons and evidence.

SAY WHAT? The **Shred It!** series from 45th Parallel Press features books about BASE jumping, rock climbing, and skydiving. Compare cliff diving to these other sports. Explain their differences and similarities.

THINK ABOUT IT! Have you heard the phrase, "If your friends jumped off a cliff, would you?" It means that peer pressure may cause people to do something risky before they're trained and ready. What do you think about this?

SEE A DIFFERENT SIDE! Why do you think cities and parks are worried about cliff diving? Why do you think parents are worried about cliff diving?

LEARN MORE

BOOK

Kelliher, Lauren. *Would You Rather...Go Skydiving or Cliff Diving?... and Other Daring Questions About Exploits, Feats, and Stunts.* Chicago, IL: World Book, Inc., 2023.

WEBSITES

With an adult, explore more online with these suggested searches.

Red Bull Cliff Diving World Series

World High Diving Federation

GLOSSARY

adrenaline (uh-DREN-uh-lin) a stress-response hormone that increases blood flow, heart rate, and breathing rate and creates feelings of strength and alertness

currents (KUR-uhnts) strong flows of water

impact (IM-pakt) the force of hitting something

obstacles (AHB-stuh-kuhlz) objects that get in the way

precision (prih-SIZH-uhn) being exact

sacred (SAY-krid) special, holy

routines (roo-TEENZ) series of repeated movements

somersaults (SUHM-ur-sawlts) flips

takeoff (TAYK-awf) jumping-off point

tides (TYEDZ) the apparent rising and falling of Earth's oceans as the planet rotates on its axis through the Moon's gravitational pull

tombstone (TOOM-stone) large, flat stone marking a grave

INDEX